EMPOWERING YOUR INTUITIVE EATING JOURNEY

EMPOWERING YOUR INTUITIVE EATING JOURNEY

GIDEON RAYBURN

CONTENTS

1 Introduction to Intuitive Eating — 1

2 Developing a Positive Body Image — 3

3 Mindful Eating Practices — 5

4 Exploring Emotional Eating — 9

5 Practical Strategies for Intuitive Eating — 13

6 The Intersection of Intuitive Eating and Health — 15

7 The Principles of Intuitive Eating — 19

8 Overcoming Common Challenges — 21

9 Building a Support System — 25

10 Celebrating Progress and Success — 27

11 Maintaining Long-Term Intuitive Eating Habits — 31

12 Navigating Social Situations — 35

13 Conclusion and Final Thoughts — 37

CHAPTER 1

Introduction to Intuitive Eating

Intuitive eating is an empowering way to make peace with food. Even those of us who have become skilled at using the 10 Principles of Intuitive Eating often struggle in the beginning stages of becoming more eating aware. A number of deeply ingrained food-related beliefs within us often share space with our desire to release ourselves from diets and feel better as eaters. But you can become more eating aware and continue releasing the power diets have had in your life.

You will improve your ability to invest eating with a fullness of purpose. So when hungry, you feed; when food lacks appeal, you stop. You will allow the joy of eating to come forward more often. Movement will become your comfort zone since you know the joy of motion lies in simply moving. You will realize health is about life not merch; your appreciation for what you earn, create, and contribute will go far beyond just simply existing in a culturally predetermined body. May your journey be a joyful one as the peace of enjoying the fruits of your labor awaits you at the end of the path.

Understanding the Basics

Imagine a life demonstrated by the unique expression of your essence and natural creativity. Can you feel the excitement of knowing that you are no longer going to be a prisoner to food prison? The bars of physical and mental restriction will be vanished. Now you are about to unleash yourself from the chains of deprivation and punishment which you imposed upon yourself, often without even realizing it. You should adopt self-discovery tools to dismantle the artificial prison which is built by diet programs, rejected by ninety-five percent or more of its inhabitants over the long term. The principles of Intuitive Eating (IE) cut through the confusion, distorted eating beliefs and flooding junk of food information. By participating in IE, you will meet and merge with your psychological, physical, and spiritual self. You will experience exciting ways to raise your consciousness about your relationship with food and incorporate constructive elements that increase your own power and control over this intimate aspect of self-care and self-supporting. With this progress, you construct your direct connection of trust with your body, respecting its trustworthiness. In this tranquil, peaceful, and joyful state of being, you are ready to become the creator of your winning body.

CHAPTER 2

Developing a Positive Body Image

Guideline 1. Use an informative tone. Positive body image is a learned asset, one that you are genetically pre-wired to achieve. However, without the type of culture in which our natural weights and shapes can assert themselves naturally, acceptance and appreciation of our genes are difficult to achieve. Sometimes, the need to see how we all fit with societal "expectations" is so great that heroic and often unnatural means are used to fit a stereotype that is not at all realistic. But whether through the last count of a diet, forced vomiting, compulsive exercise, or massive plastic surgery, the uncovering of a realistic self is all that we really want.

Guideline 2: Exclude. The closer parents stay to their natural weight and shape, and those of their mates, the easier it is for children to follow examples. Letting them find their natural paths and supporting healthy behaviors and choices are the most powerful gifts they can be given. But always feeling that they are loved, no matter what shape or size they may be, is the most powerful message of all. When we do find this body and discover all of the strengths and limitations to which it was intended, your whole intuitive eating process is significantly enhanced! The next goal in achieving a healthy life is to rid yourself of the dieting baggage in which many have indulged. In the final analysis, it leaves a body heavier and less healthy than it would have been if left alone.

Cultivating Self-Compassion

When we allow ourselves to release feelings of guilt and shame that can creep in on this journey, we make room for peace, compassion, and ultimately, genuine care for our bodies. Although it can be challenging to cultivate self-compassion, it's a critical tool for this journey. So, what does it look like? It's taking a deep breath when you need it. It's having a simple conversation with friends. It's the ability to say "no" guilt-free. As you work to maintain a mindset of growth and learning throughout this guide and your journey, sprinkle in self-care and compassion. By carrying kindness and compassion with you wherever and whenever you can, you will eventually harmonize and infuse your life with self-compassion. Be kind to yourself. Many confuse self-compassion with a lack of motivation; rather, it acts as a driving force and support for motivation. The practice of self-compassion allows us to make peace with food, even when it feels hard.

It's essential to practice self-compassion throughout your intuitive eating journey to help silence your inner critic. Self-compassion builds resilience and an emotional safety net. The kindness and understanding you give yourself by developing a practice of self-compassion fosters motivation and encouragement to move through the process of breaking free from dieting. Remind yourself that you're choosing to move into a journey that allows you the space to learn so that you can approach your relationship with food and your body with more understanding and acceptance. Spend time reflecting on your relationship with dieting and learn to catch any negative self-talk. Release it through practicing self-compassion.

CHAPTER 3

Mindful Eating Practices

Particulars or environmental cues to eat, such as mealtime and snacktime. Each meal or snack will contain carbohydrates, protein, and fat to keep you satisfied. This will ultimately help your body trust that it will be properly fueled in a short amount of time. Research suggests that establishing this sense of regularity will allow set point theory to work. This mechanism indicates that the body prefers to be at a certain weight, on the premise that it functions the best at this weight.

Enjoy what you are craving and savor your food. Try not to adhere to diet rules - remember to always eat before physical hunger turns into ravenous hunger. When you finally do eat, you inevitably eat faster and then end up consuming more than you anticipated. Start to honor your hunger signals until you are eventually able to normalize your relationship with food. There are numerous practical ways to engage in mindful eating practices, so continue to explore those that resonate with you. Please do not engage in mindful eating as a form of punishment. Allow the food to do its job of fueling and satisfying you.

You can achieve this by choosing an area to sit, taking time to chew your food, and minimizing any potential mealtime stress. Using a meal or snacktime as a break in your busy day can also allow you to digest more easily - eat food you enjoy and that gives you energy and satisfaction.

Mindful eating is about paying attention to the food we eat and our bodily sensations while eating. These practices will help you differentiate when you are physically hungry and full versus eating from an emotional place. Food tastes better and is more satisfying when you are present while eating it - create a peaceful eating environment.

Eating with Awareness

Be curious. Eating with awareness is not about creating a sense of control around eating or food choices. Instead, it is about noticing what you observe when you are eating. It is based on curiosity and noticing the details of your experience. You may want to invite yourself to become interested in finding out what you notice if you were to slow down, tune in to the sense perceptions related to eating, and then honor each observation. As you practice eating with awareness, you may notice anything from how eating slowly impacts your physical hunger or fullness experience to whether the sensation of taste changes as you continue to eat a particular food. Since the practice is based in curiosity, the possibilities for what you might notice are endless. Your observations do not need to be used as opportunities to create goals or change your eating habits. Instead, consider your observations as valuable sources of information that provide insight into what brings you satisfaction when you eat.

Eating with awareness is an essential skill for both recognizing physical hunger and noticing when your body has had enough to eat. It is based on mindful eating principles, which encourage you to experience food with all your senses. Eating with awareness does not require you to move through each step in a linear or rigid fashion, as might be required with a formal mindfulness practice. Instead, it helps you to remain present in the moment and to make choices that help you honor your hunger or satisfaction. Practicing eating with awareness can be especially helpful when you notice that your food choices are subject to rigid food rules or when you tend to eat while multitasking.

CHAPTER 4

Exploring Emotional Eating

Emotional eating is exhibited when people use food as an attempt to manage painful feelings. Instead of managing the stress in healthier ways, they often choose to resort to emotional eating, escalating an already distressing situation. Did you know that under stress, people also do not engage in healthier forms of "stress-relief" like mindfulness meditation, spending time in nature, listening to music or doing anything that feels meaningful & productive? When we are stressed, we don't make more time to exercise, commune with nature, practice mindfulness, spend quality time with friends or find out long-term solutions. The decision to choose food or other forms of emotional sustainment are often taken at the spur of the moment because of the temporary high, which thereby increases the impulsive habits. Using food to satisfy our emotional needs is not wrong. As humans, food provides sustenance and satisfaction. The primary stage of utilizing food to comfort, nurture and soothe is our primary caregiver – our mother. Using food to celebrate, as well as mourn and anchor, is partnership. It's just when stress becomes constant, the primary anchor is often seen in temporary emotional eating rather than resorting to long-lasting solutions.

Feeling stressed? Will you turn to food, booze, cigarettes, or some other substance to soothe stress? Is that emotional eating? Research by Stice, Yokum, Burger, and Rohde (2015) confirmed that individuals eat more in response to stressful events which could not be attributed to their personal lack of self-regulation. Instead, contextual variations are perceived as emotionally driven. Eating, laughing, smoking, or boozing are responses to make ourselves feel better. Did you know that all these activities have one thing in common? Every one of them lights up the same neural pleasure centers that respond to heroin, cocaine, and nicotine (the drug in tobacco).

Identifying Triggers

Understanding the myriad factors, internal and external, can impact the body's energy from mood, stress, types of food, types of movement, metabolism, gut microorganisms, nutrient status, genetics, size and anatomy of the individual's stomach and other parts of the body. These are important to incorporate without guilt, fear, or shame, as part of the decision-making process that any individual makes daily in negotiating how much and when one eats in one's own lived body. First, taking an inventory of the components of your daily life in good and complex foods that your body will thank you for with its health-giving properties of phytonutrients, fiber, omega-3 fatty acids, monounsaturated fats, slow-digesting carbs, protein, probiotics, and antioxidants.

To minimize mindless eating, it is important to recognize your triggers. What prompts you into eating when you are not physically hungry? Are there certain times of the day, certain physiological states like fatigue, and emotional eating, sheer boredom or happiness? Keep tabs on triggers and learn to be aware of and avoid becoming allostatically challenged. A goal is to decrease the amount of total daily stress on the body with the long-run goal to exert your reserves in a sparing, not spendthrift, fashion so that your integrity becomes proven.

CHAPTER 5

Practical Strategies for Intuitive Eating

You are not alone when you feel like you've failed or that you've done something wrong. You haven't! You're doing the best you can based upon the skills and tools you have at the moment. With an intuitive eating approach to life, you empower yourself to be the best you that is living not only in the moment but engaging in your life as it unfolds. You experience the joy and pleasure while creating your future.

When you begin start out on the intuitive eating journey, it can feel really challenging. It's a big shift, especially if you've been disconnected from yourself for a long time or even never really experienced being an intuitive eater. Much of what the media says is counterintuitive to your intuitive nature. It's not your fault that you've had moments where you felt lost and came out of touch with yourself. Your body has the wisdom to guide you to the life you want, the cravings for something other than food. You've heard of running or being on autopilot? It's like you were on this ride that you wanted to get off of but couldn't. Intuitive eating is the opposite of not being in touch with your needs. It's creating a balance between your mind and your body.

Meal Planning and Preparation

We realize that sometimes planning meals takes time, especially for those of you who are not used to doing it. Why question work if you can do something superior to having feedback? The fact is, meal planning and preparation can take a little time, but with practice and some support, you may learn how to keep it easy while providing your soul with the food it requires. Meal plans can also save time and energy during the week if done correctly, while providing food in moments of "need" or because we use intuition when we delay eating and start believing that we are "hungry".

Meal planning and preparation can help you energize and satisfy your soul. You may think about avoiding meal planning and eating on demand as options to decrease the possibility of disordered eating habits. Know that using meal plans can be a useful tool that allows you to stay connected to your intuitive eater while meeting the needs of catching your soul. When you get busy and overwhelmed and forget to slow down to taste your food, a meal plan can remind you that it is physically nutritious.

CHAPTER 6

The Intersection of Intuitive Eating and Health

One of the important myths of diet culture is that healthy and variety of foods are less tasty and fun. The truth is there is great taste sensation in experiencing the nuances and variations of food. Additionally, when the body is truly hungry, the best foods are those foods that will give you both pleasure and satisfaction in the vitamins and minerals that it craves. The more you eat (overeat) something, the less satisfied you will feel by it the next time. Eventually, the body (biological response) will tell you that you don't want it as much. The body will also know which textures, what tastes, which nutrients, and what mouth feel/volume will bring most satisfaction. Thus, the body wants a variety/healthy food subconsciously when engaging in intuitive eating. When the body is fully in charge, it is carefully selecting how enjoyable foods will be eaten and enjoyed.

Intuitive eating is not a weight loss program. It is a joyful, radical intention to create an agreement, a partnership, and resonance between your biology and your soul. At some point along the way, I honestly wish to say, though, I hope you have abandoned the war you once had with your body, that you have come to peace and to resonance. The connection of mind, body, and soul was always there. It has never really been about the food. It is time to come home.

Understanding the Health at Every Size (HAES) Approach

HAES discourages the use of dieting, it promotes finding joy in moving one's body and integrates an integrative model of care. Most of the HAES Approach emphasizes promoting effective health behaviors and self-care for health enhancement without using the outcome of weight. It can improve health and result in better outcomes than pursuing weight loss. We know from experiences with diets that people may lose weight, but they do not experience improvement in many health metrics, nor do they always feel better. Gaining weight back is the expected outcome. As size becomes the major focus (over health changes), other issues such as eating inequities become secondary, or worse, remain ignored. Victim blaming and discrimination can result. With its emphasis on the client-provider relationship, trust, integrity, authenticity, and a partnership between providers and their patients, the HAES Approach encourages removal of the emphasis from pursuing weight loss and instead shifts the focus on coaching, role-modeling, collaboration, and the nurturing of personal health pathways.

One problem with the use of the BMI is that the BMI score should be "thrown out" of the definition for obesity in health insurance. The use of the BMI is not appropriate until researchers can prove that the health correlates outweigh the costs of weight cycling and yo-yo dieting that accompany the majority of "successful" weight loss attempts.

The Health at Every Size (HAES) philosophy advocates: (1) accepting and recognizing that our bodies come in all shapes and sizes, that we don't have control over the size and shape of our bodies, and we can't change something we can't control; (2) promoting responsible personal care; (3) providing acceptance and respect for the size diversity that exists; (4) promoting eating in a flexible manner that values pleasure and honors the internal cues; and (5) shifting the focus from weight to health.

CHAPTER 7

The Principles of Intuitive Eating

The primary focus of intuitive eating is to stop the pursuit of weight loss through dieting (understanding that dieting triggers the opposite effect of its intentions), stop the practice of good and bad food police and adopt an approach that focuses on nourishing and nurturing our bodies in a caring relationship. Then the chapter expands by giving you the ten principles of Intuitive Eating, briefly describing the defining characteristics of the eating style we knew was buried under years of chronic dieting, rational food rules, and the moral labeling of certain foods as "good" and "bad". As we discuss each principle further in the chapter, the relationship that dieting has impeded will start to rekindle, guiding the journey toward healing your relationship with food and body. At the end of the chapter, there are gentle ways of exploring and uncovering the necessary changes, which are small, incremental steps. Your attitude toward food will gradually shift over time if you practice learning and connecting to these ten principles. The guidelines to on how to start, as well as the way that progress is perceived and integrated, are also described at the end of this chapter.

Rejecting the Diet Mentality

Recognize the diet mentality. If you feel that any food will make you thin, have obsessive thoughts and obsess about food, criticize yourself by eating certain food, feel that eating is healthy, eat out of the box, and eat when you are most hungry. Avoid high-temptation situations. Throw away magazines promoting diets. Ban destructive negative slogans. Replace them with reasonable health statements. Think positively about the message and assess its realism. Topics that interest and inspire you other than appearance. Find support. Communicate with those who respect your self-confidence and encourage positive body image.

Rejecting the diet mentality is the foundational principle of intuitive eating. Dieting leads to food preoccupation, reinforcing natural weight gain, and loss of connection with the body's own intuitive wisdom. Overly interpreting nutrition and healthcare messages can lead to reduced self-confidence and self-awareness. However, once you realize that resisting the diet mentality is the answer to being accepted, you can look for long-term lifestyle changes such as taking comfort in food, esteem, and peace with your natural body form, and health at every size. The flexibility to eat for nourishment and pleasure.

CHAPTER 8

Overcoming Common Challenges

When support from friends and family doesn't feel supportive: So what do you do when you're trying to become an intuitive eater and those around you are telling you that you're making a big mistake? For most of us, natural health patterns, clearing our heads, and reclaiming our authentic eating would draw cheers and high fives from the people who care about us. Unfortunately, this isn't always the case. If friends' and family's responses feel like roadblocks, think of what sort of support you're actually asking for and communicate your needs. Sharing only broad goals means you only get broad support. Their questions and support often say more about their curiosity, their thoughts about you, or an internal struggle they're having than they do about your choice. Remember, this is about your body and your well-being, not about justifying your choices to anyone.

Sovereignty: This week we're nailing down some key points about what it means to nourish our bodies, and we're looking at some of the most common challenges that might get in the way of that effort. The first, and absolutely most important principle to understand is that this journey belongs to you and you alone. It doesn't belong to the author of Intuitive Eating, your sister, your best friend, or the unwitting coworker who made a snide comment about your lunch. The power to make decisions about your body belongs to no one except you.

It's normal for trying to become an intuitive eater to come with a few challenges. In a culture preoccupied with dieting, it's common to run into a bit of resistance or confusion along the way. But just because it's common, that doesn't mean it's inevitable. This week we'll cover some of the most common issues that come up on the path to more freedom with food and how to take your power back.

Dealing with Food Guilt

Can you take a moment to name what made you feel guilty? For example, did you allow yourself to really enjoy cake at a special office birthday party? Did you feel negative emotions about feeling well fueled and full of energy all day after you made peace with carbs? As you think about what you felt guilty about in regards to your food choices, ask yourself if these sound similar to these examples? If so, remember that practically everyone who has ever had to eat less than they wanted in order to get to a desired weight or body shape experienced similar pangs of guilt. Whether someone loses weight or not, significant hunger outstrips the enjoyment and satisfaction of eating and results in repeatedly failing at attempts to lose weight. These are the individuals who feel like a failure even after they lost a substantial amount of weight. So remind yourself, if you are feeling guilty you are in some way, like countless others.

If you are feeling guilty about what you want to eat or what you ate, first remind yourself that you are not alone. Food guilt, unfortunately, is pervasive in our culture. We grow up with constant, covert and overt messages that tell us there are so many "good" and "bad" foods. Unless your grandmother has had many generations to forget all that she learned about food during the depression and because our culture encourages you to turn to sugar/insulin raising and craving foods due to stress and anxiety, it's likely that you grew up eating your feelings. Food may have been "good" if you ate it since you were told it was meal time. Food may have been "bad" if you ate when you were the most hungry, by taking time out to be present while eating. This you may have learned was "wasting time" because you were trained that having food ready as soon as newly arrived home from work was the only way to be a good mother, or wife.

CHAPTER 9

Building a Support System

It's important to have a variety of resources simply because accessing healthful food is also a matter of privilege, and we want ourselves, our family members, and our care providers to have a diverse understanding of food and eating in order to avoid stigma for cultural foods and practices. Our healthcare providers also bring their own trauma and cultural experiences to the table, which can impact how they provide care. A diverse group of resources can improve the overall effectiveness, care, and support your Dive discussions will elicit. With that said, you must build a stronger circle of concerning supportive allies who will help guide you through your own intuitive eating journey.

Pursuing a better relationship with food while also working to undo the effects of our collectively fatphobic culture and trust in the messages of diet culture is difficult. I wholeheartedly suggest working with a non-judgmental licensed social worker or mental health counselor trained in Health at Every Size and Intuitive Eating. You can look for someone who understands these concepts at the following sites: Dietitians for Body Trust, Hayes, Emilya K., MS, LPC,

Association for Size Diversity and Health, Association for Size Diversity and Health's Training Finder, Fat Positive Therapists.

Engaging with Like-Minded Communities

Remember to remain aware that thinking takes time and maintaining momentum in this thinking and exploring food and eating sits at the heart of your work will be of most value. After experiencing a fundamental intuitive eating activity, take a moment for some personal reflection. Time spent resolving the internal tug-of-war around your 'stop rules' is your focus. A belief-disbelief two-way conversation helps you define a stopping point that genuinely honors your psychology and biology. A repeated analysis of meal constructs builds strength and flexibility in your perception. Refocusing on your exploration of intuitive eating and its suggestions, a different activity is suggested. With your focus now on the empowerment side of intuitive eating, a centering technique is your potential gate. Practice of selective changing develops your ability to make modifications in response to physiological and emotional feedback.

After pausing to consider your deeper motivation to lead an intuitive life, it is time to enrich your understanding of what intuitive eating is and is not. This next stage can be one of many more. On your journey, you will likely return to this and the subsequent stages, gaining new insights and deepening your understanding. With the basics in the toolkit, try one of the fundamental intuitive eating activities. These are the 'Focusing on the Core Skill of Intuitive Eating' exercises and they are the building blocks of food peace. Once an exercise aligns with your current interests or struggles, take the time to carefully address each step.

CHAPTER 10

Celebrating Progress and Success

Our world is full of potentially wondrous events to marvel at, creatures to care about, and work to be done. Eating and weight concerns may have ruined your opportunity to participate, in your own unique way, whatever your ambitions or dreams are. Working toward making peace with food can eventually leave you free to pursue different desires. You can anticipate whatever adventures with your eating await you.

Certainly, the quantity of time and energy you spend around food has changed since you initiated the adventure. It is entirely possible that the time you previously devoted to preparing to eat and actually eating carefully measured quantities of food rarely actually having to think about what you were eating—interfered with other activities that might have ritualized food as much as dieting did.

If you've experienced years of fighting eating, you may not have the easy, knowing spontaneity with food someone else might. You may recognize that you had the ability to eat whenever "appropriate" (i.e., "hunger," "meal time") under anyone else's prescribed regimen. Eating in response to anything else, no matter how valid, just isn't in everyone's privileged domain.

Perhaps some time ago all the questions others raise in relation to eating would have seemed simple to you—and, if you borrowed their answers, you'd eat just like them: within a structured eating plan, according to the time of day, because you had the points to count, and so on. Because guidelines for your eating were so explicit, the maze of eating choices and possibilities beforehand may have seemed manageable.

Taking a moment to celebrate how initiating intuitive eating has allowed you to take initial steps towards making peace with food can help empower you to keep moving ahead. You might already be experiencing greater satisfaction from meals you eat in response to hunger, increased sensitivity to physiological fullness, diminished feelings of restlessness and urgency, and more.

Setting Realistic Goals

Set small, realistic, and achievable goals you can see, feel, and understand the progress of. The energy and excitement that you feel while achieving these small goals feed off each other, creating feelings of joy, suppleness, and a sense of achievement. Don't look to food or your body to see the meaning of these celebrations. Acknowledge and allow your body to take part in your awareness of your connection and the reasons why you wish to feel this way. Creating small goals is not saying you will change after "the" trip, "the" holiday, "the" diet, and so forth. Starting at home or right where you are right now ends right there — with home. With where you are right now. Just start where you are right now. Not tomorrow or the time when you have more energy, feel more vibrant, lose 10 to 20 pounds, or after a special vacation, but today at home. Not tomorrow — now! Start out simple, start out slow, and remember to pace yourself.

We live in a world that mostly focuses on quick fixes and instant gratification. Many of us have become 'wired' to expect things to happen in our lives with great speed and no patience. Empowering your journey to make peace with food is not just about issues of control or what really is important to you. It is also about patience and time. Making the choice to not diet in the usually agreed-upon forms does mean that you are on a lifelong journey. This may sound quite daunting and overwhelming, but that does not have to be the case. In this world where most of us want immediate satisfaction, you need to learn to work with the goal in front of you while focusing on the meaning of it all.

Maintaining Long-Term Intuitive Eating Habits

Maintaining long-term intuitive eating habits, however, is not the same as the aforementioned programs. Individuals need to change their behavior and then continue to practice this change to ensure long-term behavioral control of their eating habits. When working with clients/patients who have chosen to learn more about their bodies and what their personal requirements are in relationship to eating, exercise and diet, it is crucial that the professional help them sustain long-term behaviors in relationship to their food intake. Just because from a visual perspective there is really no definitive way to decipher between the person who has been trying to change his/her behaviors and the person who has been able to make the change and has been successful and satisfied with his/her eating habits, we should not forget the concept of behavioral change. It is the follow-up, long-term maintenance and/or intervention that separate successful long-term behavior changes from successful, unsatisfied short-term behavior changes.

Some behavioral change programs are periodization schedules in which there are specified lengths of time for change and the schedule is complete. For example, a periodization schedule that many of us are familiar with is a weight reduction program such as Weight Watchers. At these meetings, clients know that ultimately they will lose their desired amount of weight. Furthermore, at the end of the intervention they can forget about the rules and regulations that were integral during the weight-losing period. There is an end point for the prescribed behavior and then the clients can go back to their old habits until they are ready to start again.

Empowering your intuitive eating journey: Making peace with food - Elyse Resch, M.S.R.D., F.A.D.A. 12. Maintaining long-term intuitive eating habits. Intuitive Eating is a process-oriented paper with a heavy emphasis on behavioral change in relationship to food intake. Behavioral change and maintenance are topics that elicit much research and discussion in the fields of dietetics, nutrition, and health education. However, very few health care professionals who work with the public focus on helping clients maintain a behavioral change program after participants have completed their prescribed intervention. It almost seems that the goal is to help individuals make change for the short-term and not focus on the long-term.

Self-Reflection and Continuous Learning

Empowerment resonates into personal will and respect for what works best for you. Questions can instigate the potential in order to enhance and make clear the intuitive thoughts and inclinations that you hold. What does food or eating look like that respects biological factors that are unique to me? How do I dearth my own pleasure for food? What anticipations am I placing on myself about my food and eating habits? Women are natural philosophers. Reflect on the questions that you postulate and continue in your quest to cultivate attunement in honoring your biology and your decisions. Engaging and participating means looking over the horizon to the latest information—from research to personal discoveries. In doing so, you are better prepared to challenge your food beliefs. What are others sharing with me today that doesn't support me and is affecting my well-being, or a diminishment of my connections with people, activities, and myself? Am I mired in my food issues? Finally, how can I exercise claiming so that I am stronger in my intuition, my aspirations, my desires, grasping this nurturing relationship with food, eating, and well-being?

Intuitive eating is about your personal satisfaction and happiness. It's about becoming empowered by gaining the confidence and ability to go back to your earliest roots and trust yourself with food. You don't need to compete with anyone else in becoming an expert. We all are in various stages and scales of being experts and beginners. Now, ask yourself the following questions: Do I expect my intakes to be normal and balanced? Can I trust myself with food? What does someone who is nurturing, not deprivation prodding, and gentle look like in terms of what they eat? Do I maintain a healthy state of well-being integrated in owning my well-being? If you say "yes" to any of these questions, you are on or moving toward the path of nurturing yourself, as you fine-tune and make your own dedication to learn. Remember that reflective work is needed intermittently to remain on this food peace path. It's especially during times of stress that the non-nurturing food thoughts and beliefs can be amplified.

CHAPTER 12

Navigating Social Situations

Contribute to social situations with gratitude in mind. Show up to any celebration with this attitude of contributing, not just receiving, and seek to make memories. Rather than affirming the diet mentality and dining with guilt in mind, striving towards a balanced intuitive eating mindset and setting up boundaries and limitations of respecting your body is enough to eat a little bit of everything, rather than eating numerous helpings of dishes or triggering foods. After the party, negative emotions should not breed feelings of regret and shame. Relax, live in the moment, and leave guilt behind you.

In social situations, it is important to focus on the relationships and the underlying emotions rather than the food itself. Rather than bonding over food or drinks (food is often a part of celebrations like holidays, birthdays, and parties), focus on the emotions and the relationships. Instead of eating for the sake of eating, try to make emotional connections and memories with the people around you. Navigating your social life with this new way of thinking will be radical but also important as you continue healing your relationship with food and your body.

Eating Out Mindfully

In regards to intuitive eating, eating out is an exciting time to try new foods and cuisines, and yes, it should still feel that way. Use the menu to help you decide how hungry you are and then decide if you want an entrée, a combination of appetizers, or if just one side dish to sample the flavors is enough. Eat until you are comfortably full with the expectation that you can usually wrap up, scrap the portion, or leave it behind. Restaurant portions are known for being much larger than the typical portion size, and if you are a person like myself who does not enjoy eating leftovers or food from unknown cleanliness, it is best to ask for a to-go box at the beginning of the meal and take care of it immediately.

Dietary restrictions are common, and restaurants have been making efforts to accommodate diverse dietary needs. For example, hosting guests with multiple food restrictions may seem challenging, but with so many dietary restrictions on the rise, the thought of hosting someone who does not have a dietary restriction is the anomaly, not the other way around. That said, regardless of dietary restrictions, your hosts will likely be very clear on their meal plans and probably will appreciate having a discussion with you about your eating habits. This discussion will not only benefit you by letting your host know about your lifestyle changes, but also will provide the host comfort and decrease possible inappropriate questions from the guests about your plate full of food. Making little thoughtful accommodations in eating situations may not sound like a big deal, but it subtly helps other eaters to be aware of ways they can dine mindfully too.

CHAPTER 13

Conclusion and Final Thoughts

Do you ever find yourself outside of a diet cycle for a while and wonder if there is more to life than worrying about food and weight? Would you like to gain some tips on how to truly enjoy food and eating guilt-free? Well, asking a fish what water is, what water really tastes like, it's pretty hard for the fish to tell you because they've been living in it. As a truly intuitive eater, you are in charge of your own health. Helping you to get there is what this book, and your body, is all about.

In conclusion, we hope that the exercises in this chapter have been helpful in supporting your intuitive eating journey. This chapter has been designed to apply the principles of intuitive eating towards its most direct aim of helping you make peace with food, empowering your journey to become the intuitive eater you were born to be. Without your rebellious phase (and there is always a rebellious phase), how could you know what the other side felt like? And if you never ventured to the wrong side of rebellion, how would you know the pitfalls, traps, and illusions? Without the rebellion, where would come the wisdom from which you teach others?

Embracing Your Intuitive Eating Journey

Intuitive Eating, addresses empowering your intuitive eating journey, embracing your journey of rediscovering attunement with your body. It offers you steps for creating a solid foundation on which you can build your relationship with eating and your body. Like other forms of personal growth, making peace with food is not a quick fix. There is a high likelihood of experiencing starts and stalls, and peaks and valleys – and these are all a part of the journey. Each detour can offer life-giving knowledge that will support directions to be in your best interest, and help you find the most direct, satisfying, and compassionate path back to the basics of eating.

A quote by Dr. Kristin Neff, author of Self-Compassion: Stop Beating Yourself Up and Leave Insecurity Behind: "Your problem is not your problem; your reaction to your problem is your problem." We apply Dr. Neff's wisdom to eating and food. Eating issues are problem-solving responses to stress. Familiar food becomes co-travelers, providing temporary solutions, a means of forming companionship and creating a diversion from feeling pain. Because food has for so long been defined as the enemy – to be resisted or fought against – the solution to the problem does not lie in "finding perfect eating:" rather, a formula for success can be uncovered, which will enable all of us to cooperate, and change.

9 798330 334742